A Walk Thru the Book of

EPHESIANS

Real Power for Daily Life

Walk Thru the Bible

BakerBooks

a division of Baker Publishing Group
Grand Rapids, Michigan

© 2009 by Walk Thru the Bible

Published by Baker Books
a division of Baker Publishing Group
P.O. Box 6287, Grand Rapids, MI 49516-6287
www.bakerbooks.com

Printed in the United States of America

Library of Congress Cataloging-in-Publication Data
A walk thru the book of Ephesians : real power for daily life / Walk Thru the Bible.
   p. cm.
  Includes bibliographical references.
  ISBN 978-0-8010-7167-6 (pbk.)
  1. Bible. N.T. Ephesians—Study and teaching. 2. Bible. N.T. Ephesians—Criticism, interpretation, etc. I. Walk Thru the Bible (Educational ministry).
  BS2695.55.W36 2009
  227'.50071—dc22
                                     2008050833

Cover image: choongmin63 / iStock

Contents

Introduction 5

Session 1 The Way and the World 13
Session 2 A Greater Power 22
Session 3 Undivided 30
Session 4 Organic Construction 36
Session 5 Life in the Light 43
Session 6 The Body's Heartbeat 51
Session 7 A Higher Power 58
Session 8 Rekindle 65

Conclusion 73
Leader's Notes 75
Bibliography 77

Introduction

There's still a copy of the ticket on the wall of the den. It's framed and a little dusty but prominently displayed. Ken's windfall seven years ago wasn't a huge amount by lottery standards, but it was enough to get him out of a hole—for a time. He keeps another copy of the ticket in his wallet. It reminds him that at least on one beautiful day long ago, he was very lucky. And who knows? Maybe it will bring him luck again.

Lisa looks in the mirror every day and tells herself how beautiful she is. Some days she sounds like she almost believes it. But even when she doesn't, she makes the words come out of her mouth anyway. "People will see you the way you see yourself," someone once told her. She hopes that's true, so she practices seeing herself differently than she ever has.

Matt has been mail ordering an expensive cologne—or, as the ad called it, "a pheromone-enhanced product for men." He might as well, he figures. His looks and personality haven't won him any dates in over a year. Something has to work. Maybe this is it.

Christine is worried about her future. Will she find a job? A nicer apartment? Or, most importantly, a husband? She could probably wait for the first two to unfold on their own, but the third . . . well, she's desperate to know. And the number for that psychic hotline seems to show up on TV at oddly "coincidental" times—like when she's been thinking about her future and a phone is nearby. She's starting to wonder if it's worth a try.

Alan has been putting a huge prayer request before the Lord for three years. He's been very persistent and, by no choice of his own, very patient. Sometimes he thinks the waiting has been ordained by God, and sometimes he just thinks he must have blown it somewhere along the way. "Maybe," he says to himself, "if I become as holy as a Christian is supposed to be, God will answer." So he vows never to sin again if God will grant his request. And weekly, even daily, he's reminded that he doesn't measure up.

What do all these people have in common? They all want life to be better, and they're convinced—or want to be convinced—that a certain technique will make it so. These people aren't unusual; they represent nearly all of us in one way or another. Some of our techniques are superstitious, others mental, some mostly or partially rooted in Scripture, some thoroughly godly, and others thoroughly pagan. We have rituals, habits, tricks, routines, formulas, and all sorts of other means to influence a situation. That's because we feel out of control, and we're desperate to have some semblance of mastery over our circumstances. Mostly we're just trying to get by in a frustrating world.

Human beings are full of questions: *What does my future hold? Who will protect me and provide for me? How can I find the truth? Does truth even exist?* When we feel confused, we search for answers. And when we feel beaten down—by adverse circumstances, by the forces of fate, or simply by the unpredictable movements of everyday life—we appeal to whatever sources of help we can find. History is littered with such appeals, from the mundane to the mystical: halfhearted superstitions, good-luck charms, psychological tricks, ritual prayers and sacrifices, magical blessings and curses, mantras, horoscopes, and on and on. Trapped in the confines of a material world, we seek access to whatever's behind it. Something in us craves an alternative to our very inadequate resources. We're frustrated by our limitations, and we hunger for supernatural help.

That was certainly true in cultures of the Roman Empire, and it's just as true today. Times change, but the needs of the human heart don't. We may not appeal to the same range of gods and goddesses once revered in Greco-Roman society, but we have our ways of trying to manipulate cosmic forces too. We like to be in control or at least to have the illusion of control. The urge to take matters into our own hands is almost irresistible. So our world is still full of rituals aimed at achieving a desired result, of offerings made in exchange for divine favor, of sacred plea bargains intended to sway heavenly sympathies. And, more often than we'd like to think, these are empty appeals.

One of the strongest messages in Ephesians is that there's a right way to satisfy our urge for supernatural power to help us in the circumstances of life, and it's more powerful and effective than we might think. We don't have to live in frustration and futility anymore. Though we have long lived in a murky, confused, rebellious environment—a world separated from its Creator by its own counterfeit pursuits—our connection with our Father has been restored through the grace and the exaltation of his Son. We are no longer alienated from God or each other; we can have deep fellowship in his Spirit. We are redeemed for so much more than we've experienced in the past.

If you've ever felt like someone groping in darkness for any hint of light; if you've ever felt powerless to face the assault on your life by the world around you; if you've ever longed for a deeper connection with your heart's true home; then the book of Ephesians will have life-altering implications for you. Its truths take us out of our own limitations, seat us at the right hand of the ultimate Father, and bestow on us the family name. We've been given an entirely new wardrobe—the clothes of the kingdom of light—and empowered with all we could ever need. Our call for help has been answered.

Ephesus

Ephesus, situated on the western coast of what is now Turkey, was an enormous city—third in population behind Rome and Alexandria—that functioned essentially as the capital of the Roman Empire's Asian provinces, even though it technically was a free city independent of Rome. It was established by Greeks about 1,000 BC and survived a variety of empires—Greek, Persian, and Seleucid—before evolving into a vital Roman financial and cultural hub. As with large cosmopolitan areas today, its philosophies and trends influenced all of Asia Minor. That's one reason Paul may have spent so much time there—nearly three years, according to Acts. He knew that the impact of the gospel in such a cultural epicenter would certainly determine its impact in the region as a whole.

Though the worship of pagan gods and goddesses and the practice of magic were common throughout the empire, Ephesus was widely known as a petri dish for the magical arts and a nerve center for pagan devotion. It had an ample supply of various temples and shrines. The temple of Artemis (or Diana, her Roman name) was the main attraction—it drew devotees from across the empire—but Artemis worship, along with Roman paganism in general, involved a wide range of activities including magic spells, astrology, exorcism, and more. Artemis was considered the supremely powerful deity over cosmic forces; in order to get along in an environment swirling with spiritual activity, one would need to know how to tap into her authority. And if someone were to challenge her power . . . well, as Paul would find out, that could create quite a stir.

That's the setting for Paul's letter to the churches in and around Ephesus. He wrote to people who had been steeped in a culture that rallied against him, who had been there when he was the center of a citywide protest, and who remembered well how intimidating a dominant culture can be. They were people of light living in a city of darkness, and Paul had lived with them in that darkness for nearly three years.

With that as the background, there would be no need for any Christian to prove the existence of demons or the presence of supernatural power to a citizen of Ephesus or its surrounding areas. In fact, nearly every Gentile Christian there had come to faith in Jesus out of that strange spiritual mix. If any advice to the churches of western Asia Minor were to be relevant, it would have to take into account the rampant occultism of Roman society. An un-supernatural gospel would have no impact there.

The Ephesian church was one of the strongest in the New Testament. Paul once wrote to the Corinthians that "a great door for effective work" had opened to him in Ephesus, even though many opposed him there (1 Cor. 16:9). It was where Timothy pastored and where John the apostle and Mary the mother of Jesus eventually lived. Paul's instructions do not seem to be directed at any particular shortcoming; they come across as encouragement for his readers to continue doing what they've already been doing. His purpose is to inspire them to see the great and deep things of the Spirit of God and to live accordingly.

The Letter to the Ephesians

Paul wrote the Ephesian letter as a prisoner in Rome. The letter greets no one by name and addresses no specific situation—even the city name is left out of the earliest manuscripts—so many believe it was a circular letter to be passed around from church to church or likely even a sermon to be preached in various communities. Since Paul spent more than two years there, he had plenty of opportunity to establish or visit a network of churches. In fact, that seemed to be his strategy; he and his co-laborers would target influential population centers and promote the spread of the gospel from those centers. It only makes sense that he would write to several congregations rather than one, even if he had not personally been to every house church that would read it.

Paul was imprisoned in Rome between AD 60 and 62—after he had left Ephesus for the last time, gone to Jerusalem, lived under house arrest for two years, and then was sent to Rome on an appeal to Caesar. It had not been that long since he had seen Ephesus, but a lot had happened in the meantime. Because of the volatile nature of the spread of Christianity, Paul emphasized themes of unity between Jews and Gentiles and awareness of false teachers in most of his letters. Ephesians is no exception, though his words about false teaching are more indirect than in other writings.

The terms and phrasing Paul used in Ephesians were not random or coincidental in the least. They were specific to the culture of western Asia Minor, particularly to Ephesus and its environs, in ways most modern readers would never notice. Though the Ephesian letter is sweeping and majestic, full of depth and insight for any reader, the original context makes it more so. When the implications of Paul's words for first-century believers are understood, the implications for Christians today become all the more relevant.

Ephesians is in many ways a bird's-eye view of salvation history, from the foundation of the world to the full and final inheritance of the kingdom. It is both lofty and practical, inspiring and applicable, and deep enough to spend a lifetime exploring.

How to Use This Guide

The questions in this guide are geared to elicit every participant's input, regardless of his or her level of preparation. Obviously, the more group members prepare by reading the biblical text and the background information in the study guide, the more they will get out of it. But even in busy weeks that afford no preparation time, everyone will be able to participate in a meaningful way.

The discussion questions also allow your group quite a bit of latitude. Some groups prefer to briefly discuss the questions in order to cover as many as possible, while others focus only on one or two of them in order to have more in-depth conversations. Since this study is designed for flexibility, feel free to adapt it according to the personality and needs of your group.

Each session ends with a hypothetical situation that relates to the passage of the week. Discussion questions are provided, but group members may also want to consider role-playing the scenario or setting up a two-team debate over one or two of the questions. These exercises often cultivate insights that wouldn't come out of a typical discussion.

Regardless of how you use this material, the biblical text will always be the ultimate authority. Your discussions may take you

many places and cover many issues, but they will have the greatest impact when they begin and end with God's Word itself.
And never forget that the Spirit who inspired the Word is in
on the discussion too. May he guide it—and you—wherever
he wishes.

The Way and the World

ACTS 18–20

The chants pushed their way over the hills so relentlessly that the whole city could hear them—even a mile away at the Artemision. In fact, the famous temple was the indirect cause behind the commotion at the amphitheater. Tourists—tons of them—came not only from the provinces of Asia but also from the far reaches of the empire to seek Artemis's favor, and the new Christ cult was bad for business. It was a perfect example of how a minor problem can become a major threat if proper measures aren't taken early enough. Now the economy was under attack, and something had to change.

Demetrius, a silversmith, had seen the warning signs. As a responsible business leader, he felt obligated to gather the members of the craftsmen's guilds to expose the threat. After all, the stability of the local economy was at stake, and that was no small matter; with a population of at least 250,000 people, probably more, Ephesus was the third largest city in the Roman Empire. It wasn't hard to get the guilds to understand the problem—or to stir them to action. A few words about declining sales in temple models, goddess figurines, sacrificial animals, amulets, magic scrolls, astrological readings, and worship attire was enough evidence for any astute businessman. The implications for every proprietor were clear: fewer travelers at the temple meant less food on their family's table. In their minds, Demetrius had provided a valuable public service.

The ensuing rush into the amphitheater was everything Demetrius could have hoped for and more. It was a full-scale riot, enough bluster and chaos to intimidate any disciple of

ARTEMIS OF THE EPHESIANS

Artemis was one of the most widely worshiped deities in the Greco-Roman pantheon. Her temple in Ephesus was financially influential; it functioned essentially as a large lending bank for local businesses as well as a worship center. Her devotees variously called her Savior, Lord, and Queen of the Cosmos, and they believed she ruled not only the great supernatural powers of the universe but also the underworld—including demons and disembodied spirits. As goddess of the underworld, she was sometimes invoked to raise the dead. Her worshipers were mission-minded, establishing Artemis cults in cities from Syria to Spain. Signs of the zodiac were displayed around her neck as a symbol of her authority over fate and the astral powers. People who served Artemis often did so out of fear of the demonic realm, which Artemis, in her great strength, would be able to overcome and subdue. Paul, as he had done in Athens, apparently declared quite publicly that Artemis and other man-made idols were no gods at all (19:26).

the Way into silence, and perhaps even enough to run Paulos out of town. "Great is Artemis of the Ephesians," they chanted defiantly for two hours. The whole city was drawn into the confusion, many locals running to the twenty-five-thousand-seat theater to find out what was going on, others simply joining in the spirit of defiance without even knowing the cause. If not for a levelheaded city clerk pointing out the complete absence of any crime, not to mention the consequences of a riot under the watchful eye of Rome, the protest might even have resulted in a mob execution of two of Paulos's friends. If anything could stop the Way in its tracks, public outrage certainly would.

That pivotal scene in Ephesus captures the conflict between the kingdom of God and the cultures and systems of the world. There's a different set of priorities and values in the kingdom—eternal truth is more important than the economic well-being of a city, for example. By definition, whenever one kingdom comes, another has to go. That's always threatening to the established order: politics, religion, economy, social relationships, academics, arts and entertainment, and more. In other words, it brings an entirely different way of life. It's unsettling in any town.

Beginnings: Acts 18:19–19:7

Focus: Acts 18:19–22; 19:1–7

When Paul first arrived in Ephesus, he went to the synagogue to persuade Jewish leaders that Jesus was the Messiah. That was his typical strategy, and it made sense for several reasons: (1) as a Pharisee trained by the highly respected rabbi Gamaliel, Paul had a ready-made audience among Jewish leaders; (2) because of their knowledge of the Hebrew Scriptures and their messianic expectations, Jews would be more likely to understand

THE WAY

"The Way" is used five times in Acts—twice in the setting of Jerusalem and three times in the setting of Ephesus—without any explanation of why Christianity earned that nickname. It *could* refer to Christians' insistence on only one way of salvation, but it's probably more than that. Because it only occurs in the geographical context of major, long-term ministry situations, it probably refers to Christians' distinctive way of life. Whereas Judaism in that context emphasized theology and Roman paganism emphasized ritual, early believers adopted a radical, counter-cultural, comprehensive lifestyle change. Regardless of the term's origin, we can be sure of one thing: the Christian movement stood out in Jewish and Roman society enough to merit a descriptive title.

how Jesus fit Israel's prophecies; and (3) because Jews were the people through whom God had chosen to reveal himself, Paul felt that they deserved to hear the news of the Messiah before Gentile audiences did.

By the time Paul returned to Ephesus, a well-educated Jew named Apollos had already spent some time there teaching about Jesus. His knowledge, however, was incomplete. He and his followers knew "the baptism of John"—repentance in preparation for the kingdom of God—but had not yet experienced the Holy Spirit birthing the kingdom within them. When Paul laid hands on them, they did.

Discuss

- Paul was usually rejected by synagogue leaders very quickly in each city, which would prompt a shift in his ministry to Gentiles (at Corinth, for example; see 18:5–6). What response did he receive at first in Ephesus (see 18:20)? Why do you think he didn't jump at the invitation?

_____

_____

_____

_____

• What's the difference between being baptized into the baptism of John and being baptized in the name of Jesus? What role did the Holy Spirit play in the baptism of these disciples?

_____

_____

_____

_____

Public Persuasion: Acts 19:8–22

After teaching for three months, Paul encountered strong resistance at the synagogue and was suddenly a preacher without a forum. Because a formal venue was critical for a public speaker, Paul and the Ephesian converts had daily discussions for two years at the hall of Tyrannus. This was either the private property of a patron named Tyrannus or a public auditorium named after him—a place where anyone interested could come join the discussion after daily business was done.

Supernatural power came dramatically to the forefront in Ephesus. Remarkable healings accompanied the ministry of Paul, while some Jewish exorcists discovered that the name of Jesus didn't "work" like other names normally invoked in Ephesian magic and exorcism. The result in this series of spiritual showdowns between the powers of darkness and the Spirit of

God was a public bonfire. In mass repentance, many citizens of Ephesus threw their magic scrolls into the fire—a visible statement that when people accept Jesus, they reject whatever they used to rely on. The total value of the scrolls, Luke notes, was the equivalent of fifty thousand days' worth of labor.

Discuss

- The book of Acts does not treat sorcery and magic as ignorant superstition. It assumes a real and evil power at work in the lives of the Ephesians. Is this still relevant today? Why or why not?

  _____

  _____

  _____

  _____

- What's the difference between the Ephesians' burning of magic scrolls and book burnings imposed by the church at various times in history? Why was the voluntary nature of the act significant?

  _____

  _____

  _____

  _____

- Is your lifestyle as a Christian distinctive enough to earn a label like "the Way"?

  _____

  _____

  _____

  _____

Public Protest: Acts 19:23–41

The craftsman guilds of the city were not unaware of the bonfire. Led by Demetrius, they were eventually stirred to action. The riot in Ephesus was more than a verbal protest; it was a real danger to Paul and any other high-profile Christian. There are records even in other cities of people being put to death for disrespecting Artemis. The danger was serious enough that the disciples and even some sympathetic city leaders prevented Paul from going to the amphitheater during the riot.

The city clerk's argument was persuasive, mainly because he effectively reminded the crowd of Rome's reaction to unlawful assemblies. The protest could, if it continued, invite the Empire to take away some of the city's freedoms. That's how strongly Rome felt about riots and developing factions. There were laws for settling disputes. If they weren't observed, consequences could be severe.

- How willing are you, like Paul, to risk stirring up trouble for the sake of the gospel, if necessary? How do you think history would have changed if Paul left Ephesus after being rejected by synagogue leaders rather than persevering in spite of opposition?

_____

_____

_____

_____

The Miletan Charge: Acts 20:17–38

Focus: Acts 20:17–21, 28–31

On his way to Jerusalem (and to imprisonment), Paul called the leaders of the Ephesian church to meet him in Miletus. His words provide a lot of information about his leadership style and the character God's servants should exhibit. He reminded them of his ministry among them, particularly pointing out the opposition he faced. With great affection and tears, he exhorted his friends to continue serving in faithfulness, warned them of dangers to come, and strongly urged them to be extremely careful about those who would distort the truth. Then he told them goodbye.

- In what ways might Paul's words in Miletus apply to your church today?

_____

_____

_____

_____

A CASE STUDY

Imagine: Tourists come to your town from all around to see the ruins of a tribal shrine. Many come out of curiosity, others come to study the history or help with the ongoing archaeological research, and some even show up in indigenous robes and reenact the ancient rituals. Regardless of the reason, nearly everyone buys a trinket at your shop. But recently, business has slowed.

That's because a new sect has won many local converts and convinced them that God is not pleased with anything associated with the ancient religion. Already one hotel has closed and some of your suppliers have quit making their traditional crafts and replicas of the shrine's relics. Several museum staffers have resigned, and the town's economy is flailing. But your shop is all you've known. Your grandparents opened it when the shrine was discovered, you spent half your time there growing up while your parents worked, and now you're the proud owner and the resident expert on local lore. But unless something changes, your kids won't be following in your footsteps. The business is barely even making enough right now to put food on the table for them.

- How would you feel about the new sect? Would you listen to its teachers to find out why it's so popular, or would you feel threatened and react against it?
- If government agencies or social activists stepped in to try to stop the trend, would you support them? How vocal would you be about the new group's right to freedom of thought if your kids were hungry because of it?

A Greater Power

EPHESIANS 1

Every morning when she woke up, Maya would make an offering at the household altar—a couple of eggs, a few ripe olives, perhaps some dates, and a little wine, of course, whenever it was available. Then at the end of a long day, she'd do the same. The sacrifice was never much, but she hoped it would be enough to appease the resident spirits. It usually was; the family may not have been blessed with prosperity, but misfortune usually kept its distance. Her dreams were generally free of bad omens. And if any blessings and curses hovered in the atmosphere, waiting to find a place of rest on their appointed targets, a good standing with the spirits of the air would come in handy. These family offerings were a small price to pay; the whims of the gods were buffered by such gifts.

PAUL'S LONG SENTENCES

In Greek, Ephesians 1:3–14 is one long sentence of 202 words, and it's followed by similar sentences in 1:15–23 (170 words) and 2:1–7 (123 words). Other long sentences are found in 3:2–13; 3:14–19; 4:1–6; 4:11–16; and 6:14–20. The reader and/or listener would have felt a little out of breath after each one. The effect was certainly intended. Why?

Part of the reason can be found in a common rhetorical device of the time. Orators would amplify and emphasize inspiring thoughts with additional clauses, participles, and prepositions to extend a sentence rather than break it up. The fact that Paul did this so often in Ephesians is evidence that he might have meant it as a sermon to be preached in various churches rather than a letter to be read in them. But it also reflects the enthusiasm with which Paul carried out his ministry and the depth of the revelation God had given him. It's not hard to imagine such sweeping, majestic, run-on phrases as attempts to express the inexpressible (see 2 Cor. 12:1–4). When a heart is overwhelmed with the glory of God, this is the kind of stuff that flows out of it.

This kind of ritual behavior was typical in Roman paganism. Manipulating unseen forces was the only way to get by in the world. And because Ephesus was a center of religious tourism, this mindset was particularly acute there. Even many Jews had adopted certain magical practices, mixing them with scriptural principles and rabbinic tradition. But among Gentiles, the vast pantheon of Greco-Roman deities mingled with the magical powers of baser spirits, and the result was a very eclectic stew of beliefs.

A group of converts had come out of that stew. They had seen the miraculous power of God, which far surpassed any power that Ephesus, for all its elaborate spiritism, had ever witnessed. Some of them, having been practicing Jews, were accustomed to being marginalized by the religious culture. Others had fed off

EPHESIA GRAMMATA

The "Ephesian Letters" (*Ephesia Grammata*) are six magical terms used in concocting spells and curses, especially for the purposes of protection against demons. They were often spoken repetitively as a mantra or written on amulets sewed into garments. One ancient story tells of an Olympic wrestler who competed while wearing the *Ephesia Grammata* around his ankle. He remained undefeated until the letters were discovered and removed, after which he was easily defeated by the same opponent. These were widely perceived as powerful words and were surely in the mind of some of the first readers of Ephesians when they read about Christ being far above all powers.

that culture since birth. But through the Holy Spirit's emphatic validation of the ministry of Paul and his co-workers, these Jews and pagans left old rituals and practices—with all their accompanying fears—behind. They embraced the one power who held all others under his feet.

That power is still at work in the world and still the object of our faith. Whatever we encounter in life, Jesus is seated above it. No matter how much life seems out of control at times, it isn't. It's under the authority of the Savior who entered our world, suffered the worst we had to offer, and still wasn't conquered. Rather, he became the conqueror. Now he shares his victory with all who love him.

Every Spiritual Blessing: Ephesians 1:1–8

From prison in Rome, Paul writes to the Christian community he had lived in for nearly three years. He uses language familiar to Ephesian culture to describe what God has done for those

24

who believe in him. Verses 3–8 would be profoundly encouraging to a former pagan who had always seen deities as capricious and insensitive. Verses 4–5 and 11 would speak directly to those who had believed Artemis guided the stars and held fates and destinies in her hand. Though the terminology resonates with both Jews and pagans, the message is decidedly different—and greater—than anything offered by common cults and customs. The love, power, and wisdom of God are supreme, pervasive, and, best of all, very accessible.

These first verses set the tone for the rest of the letter/sermon. This is going to be about God's ultimate plan, the plan that's older than the human race. It is God's great pleasure to bring us into his kingdom. He loves to bless his people because that's who he is: a blesser.

Discuss

- How would verses 3–8 impact someone who had always believed the gods were capricious and insensitive? How would 4–5 and 11 impact someone who once believed Artemis guided the stars and held fates and destinies in her hand?

God bestows his good gift abundantly

Artemis looks kinda small compared to my God

_____

_____

_____

- What's the difference between impersonal fate and God's divine sovereignty? How would each affect the way a person lives?

_____

_____

_____

Isa 65:11 because you have forsaken the LORD & his Temple and worship the gods of fate & Destiny

25

Drawn Together: Ephesians 1:9–14

God's plan from the foundation of the world has been to unite all things in heaven and earth under Jesus. Gentiles need to know that this plan was revealed through Jews, and Jews need to know that the plan includes Gentiles. It may be a stretch for each group to come to grips with those facts, but they'll have to. Everyone in Christ has a new identity; that's what makes unity in him possible. Those who believe in him have been adopted into his family, with all the blessings and privileges of the family name included.

God's plan is not just theoretical or invisible; there's evidence. The Holy Spirit was given as a tangible guarantee or "pledge"—it's the same term as a down payment that obligates the purchaser to complete the transaction in the future. There's permanence in this relationship. It can't be overpowered or undone by outside forces.

Discuss

- Why do you think Paul emphasizes that God gets pleasure out of his own plan (vv. 5, 9)? Have you ever pictured or imagined God as a reluctant giver of blessings? If so, why?

Because I am

_____

_____

_____

_____

_____

_____

_____

- Paul says that our unity with Jesus implies a co-inheritance with him (v. 11). What has Jesus inherited? What does it mean, in practical terms, to share in the inheritance with him?

_____

_____

_____

_____

Eyes of the Heart: Ephesians 1:15–23

The rest of chapter 1 is a prayer—one of the most profound in Scripture. With gratitude and affection, Paul pours out his heart to his brothers and sisters in Ephesus. In many ways, they are in hostile territory with an often-confusing climate. They need supernatural vision, the ability both to discern counterfeits to the faith and to recognize the eternal treasures God gives them. Most of all, they need to know that whatever powers may seem to threaten them, it's the power that raised Jesus from the dead that works on their behalf. And everything—for all time and all places—will bow to the same Jesus who fills the church with his Spirit.

Discuss

- What specifically does Paul pray for the Ephesians? Which elements of that prayer would you most like to see answered in your life? Why?

_____

_____

_____

_____

- See how many references to "power" (and related concepts) and to "heaven" or "heavenly realms" you can find in chapter 1. Knowing what you know of Ephesus, how are these terms related to the religious culture of the city?

_____

_____

_____

_____

_____

_____

_____

_____

A Case Study

Imagine: You grew up on the streets of Lima, Peru, because your parents couldn't afford you. They took you into the city to the market with them one day, stood you in the central square, uttered a cold goodbye, and turned and walked away. It hurt, but it's a faint memory now because, after all, you were only four at the time. Now you're twelve. You've learned to survive.

But through a strange turn of events—you helped out a man with a flat tire, and the man happened to be the richest business owner in the region—you've been taken into a lavish home. He heard your story and felt compassion. The next thing you knew, you were sitting on fine upholstery, eating gourmet food, and wearing designer clothes. The servants called you by the man's last name and showed you the hundred-acre grounds, the pool, the refrigerator, and the secret rooms of the mansion. Then they said, "Make yourself at home. You're part of the family."

- How long would it take before you felt comfortable sitting on the furniture or before you quit sneaking food into your pockets at every meal because you weren't sure when you'd get kicked out?
- Why do you think many Christians aren't aware of how lavishly God has blessed us? Or *are* aware but are still suspicious of his goodness? Or wonder how long it will take to get disqualified from his favor?
- How would your life change if you really believed, deep down inside, that you were a coheir with Jesus?

Undivided

EPHESIANS 2

Early in his ministry, Billy Graham preached at a crusade in Tennessee where all whites were on one side of the auditorium and all blacks were on the other. Before one of his messages, he walked down the middle aisle and pulled down ropes that were separating the two sides. Ushers awkwardly tried to put them back up, but Graham wouldn't let them. It was a tangible way of making a scriptural point: in Christ, there is no black or white.

That message is drawn directly from Paul's teaching about Jews and Gentiles, a division that was at least as sharp in the first century as racial divisions were in the 1950s South. Gentiles were allowed to enter the outer courts of the temple in Jerusalem, but a barrier around the inner courts was inscribed with

THE CORNERSTONE

The word Paul uses in verse 20 for "cornerstone" is *akrogoniaios*—literally "extreme corner." There is some debate as to whether he meant a cornerstone of the foundation or an ornamented keystone at the top of a wall, a common and prominent element in Greco-Roman architecture. The keystone fits the image of the church growing up into Christ as the head, while the cornerstone is more consistent with the image in Isaiah 28:16 of God laying a sure foundation in Zion. And since Paul was writing to both Jewish and Gentile Christians—primarily to the latter—it's hard to say for sure.

Either way, it's a substantial metaphor. The foundation stones of the temple in Jerusalem were enormous; the largest discovered by archaeologists is 55 feet long, 14 feet thick, and 11 feet high, weighing about 570 tons. And crowning keystones were beautifully ornamented focal points for any important building. Whichever metaphor Paul meant, his main point is clear: Jesus prominently and powerfully holds two walls—Jews and Gentiles—together.

a stern warning: Gentiles who enter will have only themselves to blame for their death. In fact, this division was the cause of Paul's initial arrest in Jerusalem after having left Ephesus (Acts 21). Some Jews had seen him in the city with Trophimus and falsely accused him of bringing the Gentile into the temple with him. Paul lost his public freedom—and very nearly his life.

In Ephesians 2, Paul declares that any and all walls dividing Jews and Gentiles have been abolished in Christ. We know from the beginning of Acts 19 that many of the first Christians in Ephesus were Jews, and we know from the end of the chapter that many more of them were Gentiles. (In a cosmopolitan city like Ephesus, that would include Greeks, Romans, Egyptians, Persians, Syrians, and more.) In every "mixed" church this seemed to cause a certain amount of tension: Jews feeling somewhat entitled to higher honor as those through whom the Messiah came and Gentiles being somewhat contemptuous of the Jewish flavor of the gospel. But Paul insists that there is now only one class of people in Christ. You either have his life or you don't. And if you do, what kind of division can there be in his Spirit?

In other letters, Paul extends this unity even further, setting a precedent for us to do the same in our own cultural context. Not only is there neither Greek nor Jew, he says, but there is also no spiritual distinction between slave and free or male and female (Gal. 3:28). Whatever outward physical appearances or social distinctions we have in our world—racial, economic, gender, and so on—there is only one class of person in Christ: alive by grace through faith. Christians are called to embrace that singular identity, and the church needs to reflect it.

Salvation in a Nutshell: Ephesians 2:1–10

If you ever wanted a good, concise picture of the plan of salvation, you'll find it in these verses. The passage begins with where

THE *SHALOM* OF GOD

When the Bible speaks of peace, it means more than simply the absence of conflict. The Hebrew word *shalom* also includes fulfillment, wholeness, completeness, safety, and abundance. It's an "all is well" satisfaction with life. And though the New Testament wasn't written in Hebrew, it was written by a lot of Hebrew-thinking people—like Paul, for example, who had long been thoroughly immersed in Jewish theology. According to Paul's words in 2:14–17, Jesus not only gives us *shalom*, he himself *is* our *shalom*.

we began, and the picture isn't pretty. We were dead, subject to the ways of the world and disobedient spirits as we sinfully followed our natural, fallen inclinations. But God mercifully stepped in and brought us out of death into life, where we're seated with Christ and blessed abundantly through him. It's the ultimate rags-to-riches story—from the lowest depths to the highest heights—and no one can claim to have earned it. It's all grace and all for God's purposes.

Discuss

- According to 2:6–7, why did God reach into the depths and rescue us? In what ways is our salvation a visible drama for this age and those to come?

  _____
  _____
  _____
  _____

- Do you think verses 1–3 apply specifically to the Gentiles who came out of the pagan culture of Ephesus or to all Christians in general? Why?

  _____
  _____
  _____
  _____

Broken Barriers: Ephesians 2:11–22

Isaiah 57:19 declares, "Peace, peace, to those far and near." Paul picks up on the prophecy and applies it to an unlikely and awkward relationship—Jews and Gentiles of a very multi-ethnic city who had come to Christ from rather distinct worldviews. Now, in Christ, they are called to be one. No barriers, no awkwardness, no factions, no favorites. Where once God had called Israel to be completely separate from the beliefs and behaviors of surrounding nations, he was now calling those nations to join Israel through its Messiah.

To reinforce his message of unity in one Spirit, Paul uses three metaphors for people in God's kingdom: citizens of a nation, family members in a household, and building material for a temple. In each picture, the parts of the whole are bound together "in Christ" in a strong and permanent relationship.

Discuss

- To what extent do you feel that you fit with and function smoothly with other parts of the body of Christ?

  _____

  _____

  _____

  _____

- How economically, racially, and culturally diverse is your church? Are there any unspoken barriers that might keep someone from attending? Are there any legitimate issues over which we *should* divide with other Christians? What are they?

  _____

  _____

  _____

  _____

A CASE STUDY

Imagine: You're in the middle of a worship service, singing songs of praise to the glory of God. For a moment, you take your focus off the Lord and look at the people around you. On the row in front of you are smiling Hutus and Tutsis from Rwanda, seemingly oblivious to the fact that genocide once ravaged their nation. On the row behind you are Serbs and Bosnians enjoying each other's company in the presence of God. And on your row, much to your surprise, you sense absolutely no tension between the Arabs and Jews singing along with you.

- How unlikely does that scene seem to you? If Christ has removed all hostility between those who are in him and joined us together as the dwelling place of his Spirit, why do you think congregations aren't more like this?
- Historically, even when groups of Christians in the same city have little or no negative attitudes toward each other, they still prefer to worship with believers who are socially and culturally similar. In your opinion, why? Do you think this tendency is good or bad?

Organic Construction

EPHESIANS 3

Massive office towers can be built in less than two years, some-times even one. They require long-term planning, of course, but the actual construction can be done rather quickly. By contrast, construction of Canterbury Cathedral began in AD 597, and though the initial plans were completed in a matter of a few years, the cathedral as we know it today was completed in 1510. That's 913 years for a work-in-progress. Not all of those years in between were filled with active construction, but many were. Some building phases came in response to fires or warfare—restoration of what had been damaged. Others were simply prompted by a spiritual leader's vision of greater things. And Canterbury wasn't the only cathedral with this sort of history. Many medieval construction projects took hundreds of years to complete, each generation contributing a part that another generation would one day see in completed form. True works of art can take centuries.

In many respects, that's a picture of God's kingdom. For centuries, God has been building his people as his dwelling place on earth. Unlike most architects of medieval cathedrals, he began with a long-term, multi-phase plan, already seeing the finished product before he even began. Before the foundation of the world, he envisioned a people for his own possession. He gathered some foundation stones from the families of Abraham, brought out a choice cornerstone from the same quarry, arranged them together, and then began building with materials from all over the world. The result is a massive temple that houses his presence as he dwells among us.

With most building projects, the blueprints aren't always seen by the public. In fact, they sometimes remain hidden to anyone except the builders until construction is complete. Likewise, God's temple of human building blocks had long been a mystery until the revelation of Jesus. When his Spirit began to fill the hearts of anyone who believed, Jew or Gentile, his purposes became much clearer. He was crafting a habitation for himself that would transcend ethnic, economic, cultural, age, and gender groups. And it only makes sense; a God of manifold wisdom and multiple expressions can't be limited by a culture or ethnicity. His fullness requires a global construction project. That's what the blueprints, now revealed, call for.

The Sacred Mystery: Ephesians 3:1–13

If the readers and listeners of Ephesians wanted a demonstration of Jewish/Gentile unity, they would need to look no further than Paul. He points out that he, a Jewish Pharisee saved by Israel's

"THE MYSTERY"

"Mystery religions" were widespread throughout the Roman Empire. These secret societies required members to participate in clandestine initiation ceremonies to impart sacred wisdom of a deity or cosmic principle. This higher knowledge was the exclusive privilege of devotees, who were forbidden to divulge the group's secrets. Each sect adopted one divinity—Dionysius, Mithra, or Cybele, for example—about whom a myth of returning to life or triumphing over enemies was central. There was essentially no conflict between the mysteries and Roman paganism, so adherents could worship any number of deities in addition to the rituals and meetings of their covert community.

The prevalence of mystery religions may be one reason Paul used the word "mystery" so often in Ephesians. The word occurs nineteen times in the New Testament, and eleven of those are within Ephesians and Colossians (which was written at the same time to a similar audience). As with the mystery sects, Paul's deity was raised to life and triumphed over enemies. The distinction Paul makes is that this was history, not myth; and that the mysterious plans of God aren't secret but have been revealed for all to share. In Paul's letters, the mystery of Christ is always discussed in the context of full disclosure to the world.

Interestingly, certain cults like Jehovah's Witnesses of today often refer to these passages about "the mystery"—"sacred secret" in their translation—in their proselytizing. The implication, of course, is that only they understand the secrets God has revealed. Even a cursory look at Paul's use of the word demonstrates that the "mystery" is plain for all to see. It's the gospel itself—the amazing fact of "Christ in you, the hope of glory" (Col. 1:27) and of Jews and Gentiles being members of his body (Eph. 3:6). In other words, the revealed mystery is that we are in Christ and Christ is in us.

Messiah, is a prisoner of Christ for the sake of the Gentiles to whom he's writing. He then launches into a reminder of his calling—God's calling for him, in fact—to be a steward of the sacred mystery: Jesus is building a family, a temple, a nation to fill with his own Spirit. In a turn of salvation history that's shocking to both Jews and Gentiles, all kinds of formerly hostile people are joined as members of one body—Jesus's body—and destined to be heirs of God's rich promises.

Why has God done such a thing? To demonstrate his wisdom to all of the rulers and authorities in the invisible heavenly realms, especially those spiritual powers that rebelled against his wisdom long, long ago. In committing high treason against the Lord of Hosts, those evil entities led by Satan were actually rejecting the Lord of unfathomable love and mercy. Now they know the truth. God has revealed the mystery. He is a Redeemer of epic proportions.

One of the results of such mercy is that human beings once dead in sin and subject to wrath (2:1–3) may now approach the

THE FATHER WHO NAMES

In the ancient world, as in many cultures today, naming someone indicated authority over that person and imparted the meaning of the name to his or her life. (That's why Adam's naming of the animals in Gen. 2:19–20 was more than a linguistic game. It was also a declaration of Adam's authority.) In Ephesians 3:15, Paul is reinforcing God's authority over *every* family in heaven and earth—not just the family of Abraham and Jacob, whom he renamed to reflect his purposes. Every family—Jewish, Egyptian, Roman, Greek, Assyrian, etc.—is under his authority and can be drawn into his purposes.

Paul may also have been making an in-your-face comment about the emperor worship so common in Roman culture. Many inscriptions from the time show that the emperor was called "father of the fatherland." Paul says God is much more than that. He's father of all fatherlands ever created, whether in heaven or on earth. As such, he is more than able to strengthen his people and fulfill the extravagant promises of this passage.

Father with freedom and confidence (3:12). The word Paul uses literally means that we have "free speech" before God. In 2:18, he used the terminology of having access to a king to describe our approach to God; here he invokes a long-held ideal of Greek democracy to say that we former rebels can now speak candidly with our forgiving Father. To angelic observers both good and bad, that's astounding.

Discuss

- How do you think a first-century Jew would have felt about the gospel being shared with Gentiles? How do you think a Gentile might have felt about the Savior coming out of centuries of unfamiliar Jewish history?

  _____

  _____

  _____

  _____

  _____

- According to 3:8–11, you and your church are key players in a cosmic spectacle that has been revealed for all heaven to see. In what ways does (or should) an awareness of that fact affect how you live? What would you do differently if you sensed that rulers and authorities of the invisible realm were observing you as an example of God's wisdom?

  _____

  _____

  _____

  _____

  _____

  _____

Beyond Imagination: Ephesians 3:14–21

Because of the mind-blowing mystery that has been revealed—that human hearts can become the dwelling place of God, regardless of their background—Paul kneels before the Father. His prayer is that Christians in the Ephesian churches would be strengthened and made deeply aware of the indescribable love of Christ, that they would be overflowing with the presence of God.

The superlatives of this passage reflect God's "glorious riches" (3:16), a term that Paul perhaps drew from the environment of Ephesus. The city, after all, was a major financial hub, a port city for intercontinental trade, and the seat of many lucrative businesses. It isn't that the Christians there were of particularly high status—they possibly even tended to be more "blue collar." But the general environment was prosperous. The Artemis temple functioned as a lending institution for local professionals, and, as we've seen, the riot instigated by Demetrius in Acts 19 was fundamentally over financial issues. This was a wealthy metropolis.

Yet God's riches are infinitely greater, his power infinitely stronger, and his love infinitely more vast than any superlative Ephesus could claim. And that, Paul says—the richness of God's love and ability—is the power at work within us.

Discuss

- Which have you found harder to trust: God's *ability* to answer your requests or his *willingness* to answer them? Why? How does 3:14–21 address both of those concerns? What do you think is the ultimate purpose of God's power working within us?

A CASE STUDY

Imagine: The return address says "1600 Pennsylvania Avenue," but you have no idea why the White House would include you on its mailing list. When you open the letter and read it, you realize that an old friend is now a political insider and has remembered you for your sharp insights, remarkable objectivity, and uncommon common sense. On your friend's recommendation, the president has invited you to the Oval Office to speak freely about the perspectives of the average citizen. It's a private meeting—expenses paid, of course—and the president is all ears.

- How much time would you spend preparing for the meeting? How careful would you be with your requests? Why? How do your answers compare with your times of prayer before the King of the universe?
- In light of Ephesians 3, are there any adjustments you should make to your prayer life?

Life in the Light

EPHESIANS 4–5:20

Pavel arrived in east Asia looking every bit like the typical European tourist, but he hadn't come simply to see the sights. No, he was there for immersion: intensive language study, a new style of clothes, and a readiness to taste unusual flavors and swallow unrecognizable food. He would study Asian history, culture, and philosophy and bond with a lot of Asian friends in the process. No matter how difficult it became and no matter how long it took, he was determined to live a local lifestyle and see through local eyes. He would leave his past behind and adopt a new identity.

Paul uses the language of a dramatic cultural transition in much of Ephesians 4. Most of his readers had come out of a thoroughly pagan background, and the shift was probably pretty bumpy. Like

43

infants growing to maturity, like creatures of darkness coming into the brightest light, and like a sudden millionaire disposing of a ragged wardrobe in favor of much finer clothes, Christians are supposed to be changed. That change applies to inner thoughts and feelings, to outward behaviors, and to interpersonal relationships. It's more than an overhaul of the soul. It's a supernaturally new self that reflects the heart and holiness of God.

That's the gospel, at least in practical terms. We're like permanent exchange students immersing ourselves in the culture of the kingdom. The big picture of the gospel has already been given in the first three chapters of Ephesians, but the fourth

HE LED CAPTIVES

In ancient warfare, victorious kings humiliated the warriors they conquered by binding them together, stripping their bodies and shaving their heads, marching them off into captivity, and dividing the spoils among their own soldiers. (Isaiah 20:4 is one picture of this: "The king of Assyria will lead away stripped and barefoot the Egyptian captives and Cushite exiles, young and old, with buttocks bared—to Egypt's shame.") Roman generals and emperors had a similar practice, usually parading a captive king (often with an embarrassing lack of clothing) into a public square and executing him before the masses. The point was to prove the power of the conquerors and shame their defeated rivals as a deterrent to other resisters.

This image shows up in one of Israel's victory songs, a messianic prophecy of God's ultimate triumph (Ps. 68:18), and Paul uses the word picture in Ephesians 4:8 and Colossians 2:15 for Jesus's victory. Satan and his hordes were decisively defeated by the cross and resurrection. Jesus humiliated the princes of darkness in the public square of heavenly realms and is dragging them off into captivity. And, in spite of the fact that we had nothing to do with helping him to victory, he is distributing the spoils of war (spiritual gifts) to his people.

and fifth zoom in on how "the Way" is supposed to play out in our lives. This is how Christians are meant to walk through a spiritually hazardous landscape.

Worthy: Ephesians 4:1–16

Paul has written of God's awesome power, his ultimate purposes, his kind intentions, and the richness of his love and mercy. And he has declared our free access to all of the above—including the fact that these lavish blessings are working within us even now. So what's the point? How does he want the churches of Ephesus and beyond to apply such dramatic, unlimited resources? They are to use the extravagance of God by walking in a manner worthy of their calling.

In other words, one of the primary purposes in having access to the strength and glory of God is for us to apply it to ourselves. The cosmic power has been planted within us—it's an internal revolution working its way outward. A new heart will develop new perspectives and new ways of relating to people. There will be humility, gentleness, patience, love, and therefore unity. We're being completely filled and equipped with the character and works of the one who has conquered every rebellious spirit in the universe.

Discuss

- What kinds of things do you think Paul has in mind when he says to "make every effort" to keep the unity of the Spirit? What does it mean to "speak the truth in love"?

_____

_____

_____

_____

45

THE GENTILE LIFESTYLE

Greek and Roman gods demanded loyalty, sacrifices, and worship, but they seemed to care little about personal morality. Society in general insisted on a certain behavioral ethic for the common good, of course, but because most deities were morally neutral, there was quite a bit of tolerance for a variety of sexual and other personal behaviors. In fact, in some pagan sects and cults, worship could involve any combination of ceremonial prostitution, orgiastic rites, and drunken frenzies. Paul's words in Ephesians 4–5 to the former pagans of Asia reflect the peace and sobriety of God's Spirit.

With regard to attitudes and character, Roman ideals emphasized duty, loyalty, cunning, a sense of honor (avenging it when necessary), and influence (through status and/or the art of persuasive rhetoric). Vigilante justice was not unusual, and retaliation for personal offenses was expected. Therefore, anger wasn't associated with sinfulness, humility was a sign of weakness rather than a virtue, and patience and gentleness weren't especially respected. So when Paul described the new clothes of the Christian, he was clearly urging his readers to defy the fashions of the day.

• How well do you balance these two necessities—truth and love—in your relationships?

_____

_____

_____

_____

Escape from Futility: Ephesians 4:17–32

"I tell you this, and insist on it in the Lord, that you must. . . ." You don't use words that strong unless you're setting up something absolutely imperative. So what is Paul so insistent about?

the exodus from darkness into light. The pagan way of life is absolutely futile. It's full of persuasive lies and false philosophies (4:14); hard-heartedness, numbness toward spiritual truth, and relentless but empty sensuality (4:18–19); dishonest relationships, angry outbursts, and a tendency to exploit others rather than earn an honest living (4:25–28); and indecent comments, bitter feelings, competitive agendas, broken (or even violent) relationships, and malicious words (4:29–32).

That's a clear description of the culture of a fallen world, but the passage also describes the culture of the kingdom: pure devotion, honest intentions, kindness, compassion, gracious attitudes, and everything else that flows from selfless love.

- In what ways does Paul's description of the Gentile way of life fit our world today? How well does his description of the kingdom way of life fit our churches?

  _____

  _____

  _____

  _____

- Statistics reveal very little ethical and moral difference between Christians and non-Christians in the U.S., and many other countries. Why do you think that is? What should be done to encourage believers to walk in a manner more worthy of our calling, particularly in our love for others? To what extent are we known in our society for our extraordinary love?

  _____

  _____

  _____

  _____

In His Image: Ephesians 5:1–20

What should the Christian life look like? "Be imitators of God" (5:1). That pretty much covers it. Our highest calling is to be the spitting image of our Father—apples that fall very, very close to the tree. Above all, that means sacrificial love, but there's more. Paul goes on to elaborate on the difference between the darkness of a world subject to futility and frustration and the light of the kingdom of Jesus. Specifically, the environment we came from is full of impurity, immorality, greed, rough talk, obscenity, drunkenness, and all kinds of foolishness. The sad result is a relentless pursuit of things such as money, sex, and power. That's idolatry—the worship of unworthy God-substitutes—and it's the kingdom we came from.

But then there's the kingdom of light, where things are made right. It's full of goodness, purity, justice, and truth. When we lived in the kingdom of darkness, we couldn't see either kingdom for what it is. As children of light, however, we can see both. And realizing the stark contrast between where we are and where we came from should fill our mouths with words of gratitude. What flows from our hearts is a melody of the Spirit that gives glory to God and builds up our fellow believers.

Discuss

- Children of light are told to "have nothing to do with the fruitless deeds of darkness, but rather expose them." In practical terms, how should that play out in our lives?

_____

_____

_____

_____

- Paul says in 5:15 to be very careful about how we live—literally, "to watch our walk with exactness." What are some areas in which you need to do that?

  _____

  _____

  _____

  _____

  _____

A CASE STUDY

Imagine: You grew up in a slum, were wounded in numerous turf wars, developed quite a few addictions to illegal substances, and even did time for stealing a car. But that's all in the past. One day in prison, you told Jesus that you'd made a mess of your life and figured he could do a better job of it. So you gave your life to him. Ever since, you've been a different person.

But just because Jesus is in your heart doesn't mean the culture of the street left without a fight. Those former addictions still call your name sometimes. So do your old friends from the neighborhood. And your record . . . well, it has a tendency to follow you wherever you go. As much as you've put your old ways behind you, they still remind you that they were once your master. You constantly have to be on guard.

- How careful do you need be to stay away from your old neighborhood? If you need to help others still in that environment—and you almost certainly will—how should you protect yourself?

- Do Christians need to stay away from "the old neighborhood" from which we were redeemed or go back to it to get others out? To what degree can a Christian be *in* the world without being *of* the world? How do we know where to draw the line?

The Body's Heartbeat

EPHESIANS 5:21–6:9

"I grew up in a dysfunctional family." That statement comes from regret—a sad lament from someone who has longed for a typical family. But dysfunction *is* typical, isn't it? That regret can legitimately be expressed by virtually anyone. To some degree, every household has a measure of dysfunction—of unhealthy relationships and unresolved issues. Emotional baggage is a fact of life in a fallen world.

Life in Christ is all about relationships, which is why the two greatest commandments are relational: we're to love the Lord with everything in us and love our neighbors as ourselves. If someone has flawless doctrine and a long résumé of good deeds but doesn't have strong, loving relationships, that person isn't exactly living the Christian life. (In fact, that's basically Paul's argument in 1 Corinthians 13, the well-known "love chapter.") It isn't possible to be "in Christ" while being continually "out of sorts" with the people around us.

THE MYSTERY OF MARRIAGE

In Genesis, God took one flesh (Adam) and divided it into two people (Adam and Eve). Then he joined two together as one and told them to be fruitful and multiply. Ever since, men and women have joined together in voluntary union to share the most intimate of loves and to expand their love through children.

That, according to Ephesians, is a picture of an even greater relationship. God brought the church out of Jesus's side, joined us with him through the Holy Spirit, and told us to be fruitful and multiply—to go into the world and bring others into our loving union. If the illustration is any indication, our relationship with him is to be deeply personal and intimate. And like marriage, becoming part of Christ's body is voluntary. So if marriage is to serve as an accurate picture of the greater relationship, it has to involve radical sacrifice on the parts of both the bridegroom and the bride. Otherwise, it can turn into just a conventional attempt at self-fulfillment.

The Sinai covenant in Exodus has long been seen by Jewish rabbis as a betrothal between God and his people. The prophets referred to Israel's idolatry as "adultery." The Song of Songs has been interpreted for centuries by Jewish and Christian theologians as a picture of God's relationship with those he loves. And, according to Revelation 19 and 21, all of history will climax with a wedding between Jesus and his bride. In the meantime, individual men and women have an extraordinary opportunity to become a small picture of that glorious relationship. It's one of the primary reasons we were made "in his image."

That's why Ephesians, so focused on the power of the Spirit, the lifestyle of the believer, and the *shalom* of God's kingdom, offers deep lessons on the *shalom* of a home. A typical household in Roman society was based on the nuclear family, but it might also include any number of extended family members and, depending on the wealth of the family, servants and slaves. And among those, there were varying levels of servitude. Regardless of the size of the household, however, or what century that household is in, people who live together have issues—and God can resolve any of them.

How would Jesus behave in your home? That's our template. That's what it means to be "imitators of God." The characteristics that God would display—or that he *did* display in Christ—form the prototype we're supposed to follow. Our relationships are to look like his.

One Flesh: Ephesians 5:21–32

"For the slave has no deliberative faculty at all; the woman has, but it is without authority, and the child has, but it is immature. . . . The courage of a man is shown in commanding, of a woman in obeying. . . . As the poet says of women, 'Silence is a woman's glory.'"

These are the words of renowned Greek philosopher Aristotle, who lived more than three centuries before Christ. Though a 21st-century worldview may see Paul's instructions for household relationships as unenlightened, they were considered rather progressive at the time—liberating, in fact. And when the meaning of this passage is really understood, Paul doesn't come across as unenlightened at all. He acknowledges the moral responsibility of each member of the household—not a commonly held assumption—and affirms that everyone, regardless of his or her social position, is equally a servant of the Lord. This was a revolutionary view.

Paul sets up his instruction with an overview statement: "Submit to one another out of reverence to Christ" (5:21). Before beginning any discussion of specific roles, the general climate has to be established. The pervasive attitude among Christians, whether at church or in the home, needs to be characterized

SLAVERY

When we think of slavery, we generally picture the brutality and severe oppression of Western colonialism. While such severity wasn't unheard of in the Roman Empire, it was the exception. There were significant differences between Roman slavery and, for example, the slavery of the eighteenth- and nineteenth-century Americas. In the empire:

- Slaves were temporary; most would be freed after a defined term of faithful service. Many earned money to buy their own freedom.
- Slavery was a non-racial issue—people of any race could own slaves, and people of any race could be slaves. Ethnic subjugation wasn't the issue.
- Tasks ranged from hard labor to household management and tutoring. Some slaves may have been treated as animals, but many were as highly esteemed as members of the family. Many chose to remain with a family even after freedom was offered.
- Free workers were known to sell themselves into slavery—sometimes because of debt, but often simply because the living conditions were better.

None of this implies that God has ordained slavery as a godly institution, of course—far from it. But in general, Roman slavery was not nearly as oppressive as the slavery exercised by Western powers in the last few centuries. It was therefore not seen as an urgent, offensive evil for the church to deal with.

by mutual submission. Power struggles are not appropriate in Christian relationships.

The first human relationship, both in this passage and in the Bible overall, is marriage. Paul's instruction for wives to submit to their husband isn't unusual for the cultures of his day, though the tone of it certainly is. Other Greek writers instruct husbands to rule their wives; Paul, on the other hand, instructs husbands to love their wives as Christ loves the church—radically sacrificially, in other words—and as he loves his own body.

The husband has an enormous responsibility. That instruction in 5:1 to be imitators of God carries over especially to married men. And there's much more than a smooth-functioning household and a fulfilling relationship at stake. This is a picture of a greater relationship: the love Jesus has for his people and the identity of his people as members of his own body. This, says Paul, is a profound mystery.

Discuss

- How do you view Paul's suggestions for marriage in this passage? Do you see them as statements on which partner is more competent to lead or as a distinction between the roles of two equally important people?

  _____

  _____

  _____

  _____

- Paul's instructions work perfectly when both parties are living up to them. How should you respond when you're doing your part and the other person isn't?

  _____

  _____

  _____

  _____

Higher Authority: Ephesians 6:1–9

Again, Paul doesn't address the head of the household first and tell him how he's supposed to rule. He addresses the children themselves, and he also gives them an incentive for their obedience: God packaged the commandment about honoring parents with a promise. As for fathers, the point of parenting is not merely to teach obedience; it's to cultivate disciples from an early age. Therefore, the spirit and attitude behind a child's training is as important as the training itself.

Even more remarkable is Paul's instruction to slaves. Why address someone who has no choice about anything? Because while slaves may be the least valued members of a household, they are as equally valued as their masters in the kingdom of God. Powerless in social structures, they are as powerfully seated with Christ as any other believer. And they *do* have a choice about some things. They can obey grudgingly or wholeheartedly. They can represent the Spirit of the Lord or the spirit of the world. Ultimately, they only serve one Master.

Why didn't Paul take the opportunity to condemn slavery? Because he was addressing people who had to live within the structure of society right then and there, not making a statement about changing a culture. Christian slaves needed to know how to exercise their new faith in the household. And if a community of believers is characterized by the mutual submission of each member, then slavery takes on a whole different flavor. Masters were to remember that they themselves are servants of a greater Master—and that God does not play favorites.

Discuss

- How does being rooted in the love of Jesus and filled to overflowing with his Spirit make it possible and even desirable for us to drop our personal agendas and submit to others?

_____

_____

_____

_____

- How does the gospel address dysfunctional relationships? Are there any relationship dynamics it doesn't address?

_____

_____

_____

_____

A CASE STUDY

Imagine: You live in constant subjection to unreasonable people—people who have power over you and know how to use it. You had such different dreams for your life, but your circumstances seem to have conspired to beat you down. As a result, every area of life has become joyless drudgery. You long to be out from under your circumstances, but you can't see it happening anytime soon. For now, you just have to learn to live with them.

- What would you do if the situation above is an unfulfilling work environment? A disruptive parent-child relationship? An abusive marriage?
- Under what conditions do you think it's appropriate for a Christian not to have a submissive attitude? Why?

A Higher Power

EPHESIANS 6:10–23

The city seemed peaceful, but it was a fragile peace. One never knew when a sniper would open fire or a suicide bomber would step on a bus. It was only a matter of time until someone walked through a booby-trapped doorway or turned an ignition wired with enough explosives to destroy a building. Yes, peace was in the eye of the beholder. And most beholders knew it wouldn't last.

Most of us don't live with the kind of alertness required in a terrorist-infested environment, but if we could see into the heavenly realms Paul describes, we would. We'd see false belief systems smothering entire cultures, poisonous lies spilling out over airwaves and even in our own conversations, and a multitude of broken relationships that were once fulfilling and meaningful until a saboteur got wind of them. We'd see a landscape littered with evil agendas and shrouded with fear and despair. Most of all, we'd see vehement opposition against the gospel of truth and tormented minds that don't even believe truth exists.

Such was the spiritual climate in which the Ephesians lived. Many of the people reading or hearing this letter had likely practiced sorcery, astrology, or witchcraft in the past. Nearly all had participated in some form of god- or goddess-worship at one time or another. But the kingdom of darkness doesn't let go of its members without a fight. Its minions know how to harass, mock, deceive, sabotage, tempt, and intimidate those who have come out of it. The war for a soul may have already been lost, but that soul's effectiveness in the kingdom of light is still up for grabs. And if a soul can be distracted from the true picture of its own redemption and the power that's available in Christ, that's worth fighting for. Believers in Ephesus faced an angry host of defeated spirits.

That's essentially the climate we live in too. Obviously our sinful nature plays a huge role in the ills of this world; not everything can be "blamed on the devil." But the sinful nature of human beings has a partner in crime—quite a few of them, in fact. They are unholy spirits, trespassers on blood-bought property of the resurrected Lord, and it's our job to stand firm against them. We who are being filled to the full measure of Christ are not destined to be victims. We're called to overcome.

The Powers of This Dark World: Ephesians 6:10–18

Paul has strained for words meaningful enough describe the awesome power of God. Now he says to be strong in it—to

THE ARMOR

Isaiah wrote of God's warfare. "Righteousness will be his belt" (11:5); "he made my mouth like a sharpened sword" (49:2); "how beautiful on the mountains are the feet of those who bring good news . . . who proclaim salvation" (52:7); "he put on righteousness as his breastplate, and the helmet of salvation on his head" (59:17). This prophet saw a God who was armed for battle.

Paul applied God's armor to the believers of Ephesus. The terms he used in Ephesians 6 were full of meaning for Jewish readers and easily pictured by Gentiles, as everyone would have been familiar with the armor of a Roman soldier, whether well-versed in Isaiah's imagery or not. Regardless of the picture in Paul's mind, the point is the same: truth, righteousness, proclaiming the gospel, faith, salvation, and the Word of God are essential for living in a hostile environment. And prayer in the Spirit must cover everything we do.

stand firm, not in our own strength but in the Lord. This is where being seated with Christ becomes extremely relevant. When someone comes face to face with the powers of darkness, it's good to know our position above them.

We're in an intense struggle—literally, a wrestling match. Greco-Roman wrestling, popular in Ephesus, was an up-close, hand-to-hand combat requiring constant exertion and concentration. This is the image Paul chose for our encounters with the kingdom of darkness, and he's clear that we're not fighting flesh and blood, no matter what human faces we see in our conflicts. No, we're wrestling with "world powers"—the *kosmokratores*, a word used in both Greek and Jewish magical and astrological texts to refer to various gods and astral powers. Stand strong against them, Paul urges. The spiritual climate of Ephesus may have appeared to focus on meaningless statues and random incantations, and opposition may have seemed to come from temple artisans and civic leaders, but Paul calls it all demonic. This is a spiritual war.

Discuss

- Practically speaking, what does it mean to "be strong in the Lord and in the strength of his might"?

  _____

  _____

  _____

  _____

- How do we know when to see our struggles as a difficult set of circumstances, when to see them as a product of our sin or someone else's, and when to see them as an encounter with invisible forces? To what degree can these influences overlap?

  _____

  _____

  _____

  _____

A Devastating Weapon: Ephesians 6:19–24

Often lost in a delineation of military metaphors is the goal of the passage: to pray. It's a repeated and urgent request. "With *all* prayer and petition pray at *all* times in the Spirit, and with this in view, be on the alert with *all* perseverance and petition for *all* the saints, and pray on my behalf" (6:18–19). In less than one sentence, there are four "alls" and five references to prayer, along with a plea to persevere.

SIT, WALK, STAND

In the 1930s, Chinese pastor Watchman Nee preached a series of messages now compiled in a small commentary on Ephesians entitled *Sit, Walk, Stand*. Regardless of some controversial aspects of Nee's perspectives, his division of Ephesians into three distinct sections is an interesting scheme for understanding its message. Each section is based on a position of believer who is "in Christ." Our first posture is being seated with Christ in heavenly realms (2:6); we have to understand who we are and, more importantly, who we're related to before anything else in the Christian life. Then comes walking as a Christian, the posture introduced in 4:1 (some Bible versions translate the Greek word for "walk" more figuratively as "live"). In other words, how do we live in light of who we are in Christ? In chapter 6, Paul explains the importance of standing our ground in our battle against the schemes of Satan and his minions. When we understand our life in Christ in that order—*seated* in his authority, then *walking* in his Spirit, then *standing* firm against his enemies—we become effective, fruitful believers.

And Paul isn't shy about asking for prayer for himself. After all, he's a member of the kingdom of light, a minister of a mystery now revealed, and an enemy of spiritual forces that would much prefer to keep the mystery shrouded in darkness. That's almost asking for repercussions from unseen powers. And, as one might gather from Paul's requests for boldness, it's an intimidating position to be in. There's only one overriding strategy for that mission: prayer.

We may not know why prayer is such a priority in the kingdom of God, but we can't argue with the fact that it is. God has chosen to accomplish his purposes in the context of a relationship with us. There are some things he will not do unilaterally. We have to ask. And sometimes we have to ask a lot.

- What do you think would have happened in Paul's ministry if people weren't praying for him? What could have happened if people had prayed more?

  _____

  _____

  _____

  _____

  _____

- How long should we persevere in our petitions without seeing an answer? How do we know when to stop?

  _____

  _____

  _____

  _____

  _____

A Case Study

Imagine: You boldly (and somewhat carelessly) told someone about Jesus in a country that frowns on that sort of thing. Now you're sitting in jail awaiting a trial that, for all indications, may not happen for months or even years.

- Would you be more likely to attribute your imprisonment to your unawareness of the laws and customs of the land; the closed-mindedness of the people who arrested you; or demonic forces in invisible realms? Why?

- Which of the following would fill your mind most: the power of Christ to overcome your guilt for getting yourself into this mess; the power of Christ to overcome such blatant injustice; the power of Christ to open prison doors; or the power of Christ to use you as a bold witness among people who have never heard the gospel? Why?

- What purposes might God have for your circumstances? Why do you think he allows his people to go through such intense struggles?

Rekindle

REVELATION 2:1–7

It was so exciting at first. Just one glance of her eyes would make his heart catapult into his throat. Her spine would tingle at the sound of his voice alone. They were made for each other, and they knew it. Their love was extraordinary, maybe even unprecedented in the annals of romance. It would never grow cold.

But isn't that what love does? The love itself may never die, but the excitement of it often does. And when that happens—when enthusiasm and devotion wane—a relationship can turn into nothing more than a set of predictable routines. Some couples call that "comfortable." Others call it a slow, painful disappointment.

That's true not only for human relationships but for spiritual ones too. History is full of individuals, churches, and movements that started out like a wildfire and ended as a pile of ashes.

MOVEMENTS IMMOBILIZED

It's a repeated phenomenon throughout church history. One or more voices of prophets or reformers spark a movement, and the movement spreads. Multitudes are impacted. A revival is born.

Then, after the first generation is no longer around—or sometimes even before—the numbers get large enough that certain standards have to be defined. The movement needs a shape and some systems. Its leaders form their own institutions to carry out the mission and to educate the next generation in the ways of God. Because certain distortions have crept in, doctrine becomes more and more precise. Soon the movement has an honored history and carries on its traditions. Then one day, another prophet or reformer comes along and sparks another movement and multitudes are impacted.

We can see this throughout the ages: The dynamics of Acts were replaced by the institutionalization of its churches. St. Francis and St. Dominic and their early followers were radicals, but soon Franciscans and Dominicans became established orders—from which other dynamic sects branched out. The Protestant Reformation was a powerful and dynamic movement that soon developed into highly structured denominations—from which other movements sprang: Wesleyanism, the Great Awakening and other revivals, charismatic Christianity, and more. When a move of God is formalized, new movements of God seem to find expression in breaking out of the formalities.

New movements and revivals eventually beg for structure, and structures eventually beg for revival. To this point in church history, that has been an inescapable dynamic. Jesus's words to the church at Ephesus seem to have been prompted by the very beginning of one of those cycles. The structure that grew up from a genuine move of God in Ephesus was starting to become only that: a structure.

We have the unfortunate tendency of trying to cage whatever God does in our lives, and the result is a lot of structures that can't contain the wind of the Spirit no matter how hard they try. But the structures remain—in our congregations, in our relationships, and in our hearts. Love gives way to the proper forms much too often.

Paul wrote of the "profound mystery" of the love between Jesus and his bride, the church. It's a marriage literally made in heaven. But somewhere between a letter from Paul and a revelation to John, Ephesus lost its love. The church was right on target with its doctrine and was was zealous about defending it. And, on top of that, its people were actively performing good deeds, apparently walking in those works God had prepared in advance for them. But there was a serious problem: their love had grown cold. Their new spiritual relationships with God and each other weren't so new anymore, and no amount of doctrine and works could compensate. Though it may be possible to have a congregation with lots of truth and no love, it isn't possible to function as the body of Christ that way. Unless they found their first love again, this church would dissolve. That's what happens when a relationship departs from its purpose and loses its joy.

Love Lost: Revelation 2:1–7

In a religious stew like Ephesus, it's important to be able to discern the right flavor. The area was rife with potential heresies as errant Christians borrowed from the culture's occultism, pagan worship, Jewish lore, and other deviations from truth. The opportunities for mix-and-match doctrine were far too plentiful.

Paul seemed to be aware of this potential early on; when he called the leaders of the Ephesian churches to meet him on

WHAT HAPPENED TO EPHESUS?

Apparently the Ephesian Christians remained strong in their doctrinal purity. Ignatius, the bishop of Antioch who was martyred in AD 107, commended them for it in one of his letters. Whether the church stirred up its first love after John's vision in Revelation, however, is unknown.

Ephesus is still a tourist destination, but not because of its religious, cultural, and economic vitality. The once-vibrant port city is now a ruin on the coast of Asia Minor near Selçuk, Turkey. One reason is that the coastline has changed; sediment from the Cayster River constantly reshaped the harbor. Two centuries before Ephesians was written, and again within a decade of Paul's letter, the harbor was dredged and the city was spared for a time. Eventually, however, natural processes were allowed to continue uncontested. It gradually declined over the course of the first millennium AD, suffering damage from an earthquake, Arab attacks, and economic hardships. The ruins of the city now sit six miles from the Mediterranean.

his way to Jerusalem, he predicted that savage wolves would come in, even from their own fellowship, distorting the truth and leading people astray. His words must have come true, and the Ephesians seemed to have passed the test. They had tested the claims of "apostles" among them and found them to be false (2:2). But in speaking the truth in love, they had apparently majored on truth and neglected love. Perhaps the cultural melting pot environment had set them on edge against doctrinal impurity—and for that, Jesus commends them. But the church doesn't represent him well unless it majors on both truth *and* love. And that's where the church at Ephesus was lacking.

The remedy, said Jesus, was to remember their first love and repent for losing it. If not, he would remove their lampstand.

In other words, they would no longer have any influence on their world. The power of God's presence would no longer be made manifest among them. The church would dissolve.

Discuss

- As you reflect on these verses, consider this: as Jesus walks among his churches, what do you think he would say about yours?

  _____

  _____

  _____

  _____

- Practically, what can a church do to recapture and cultivate its love for God? For one another? How effective are our outward attempts at renovating our inward dispositions? Why?

  _____

  _____

  _____

  _____

A CASE STUDY

Imagine: As an expert in Christian apologetics, you've been invited to participate in a debate about religious beliefs and, having very strong opinions about the one true faith, you accept. Joining you in the debate will be a Hindu mystic, an Orthodox rabbi, a Wiccan priestess, an atheist attorney with a long record of lawsuits against Christian expression, a zealous Muslim imam, a Buddhist monk, a high priest of Satan, a Zen master, and a highly educated agnostic philosopher. You are the lone Christian voice. A talk show host known for his ability to touch raw nerves and provoke strong responses from his guests will be the moderator.

You know that some of the debaters are sympathetic toward Christian beliefs, but you're very concerned about others who have a reputation for insulting Christians. And your concerns turn out to be valid; as the debate progresses, it seems that the most vocal participants are more interested in tearing down your faith than proving their own. They exaggerate your points in order to mock them, and they blatantly misrepresent your views in order to disprove them. They even throw in a few lies about your past, calling you a hypocrite and accusing you of cultural insensitivity. But fairly regularly during the volatile conversation, the host quiets the combatants, turns to you, and says, "Let's see how the Christian responds." And you've been waiting for those moments because you know exactly how to refute the arguments leveled against Christianity. Being equipped with an answer has never been your problem.

- What attitude will you convey when you speak your mind? Would you address the personal insults and lies or just let them slide? Would your rhetoric and the spirit of your words reflect the contentiousness of the debate?

- In what ways is this scenario representative of the culture at large?
- In your opinion, how well do Christians who speak of religious issues in public balance their expression of truth with their expression of love?

Conclusion

We once were lost but now are found. And more than simply found: we've been adopted into the royal family, clothed with royal clothes, and given the royal name, which we have permission to use liberally. And, come to find out, our adoption was planned from ages past. Our lostness was a brief anomaly, now remedied forever. We don't have to wonder where we are; we're in the ultimate throne room.

We were also once blind, but now we see. And more than simply see: an entire kingdom of light surrounds us—even when we have to step back into the darkness for the sake of those we love. We see realms that were once invisible not only to our eyes but to our spirits, but now our spirits know the battle that rages there. And high above, we see feet of the one who conquered every enemy and reigns over them all.

It's extremely important to be aware of these things as we walk through this present darkness. Our destiny was no accident; it was God's deep pleasure. Our spiritual poverty is no hindrance; his riches are freely given. Our weakness isn't weakness; it's simply a platform for him to display his power. Our relationships aren't just interactions with people; they are snapshots of the eternal kingdom and building blocks of God's earthly residence. And our prayers aren't just a spiritual discipline; they are our lifeline in a brutal struggle between God and the venomous, spiteful spirits that hate his kingdom.

So what are we to do? See with the eyes of our heart, understand who we are, put on Jesus as if he's a new set of clothes, and fight intense battles as if we have the upper hand. That's what it takes in any culture in any age. The world is a minefield. It swarms with influences that would deceive us or sabotage us, and Ephesians is something of a field manual. If we follow it, we can't be defeated. It shows us who reigns—and how we can reign with him. It reminds us that we have everything we need to get by in this world.

Leader's Notes

Session 1

The Bible reading and commentary text in this session are much longer than what you will find in other sessions, but this background will be rewarding if your group can take the time to cover it. Encourage members to read as much as possible before coming so you'll be able to cover as many discussion questions as possible. If you are pressed for time, however, consider briefly summarizing the section called "Beginnings" without discussing the related questions. The remaining segments of the session give much more background into the situation in Ephesus and are therefore more directly relevant to the letter of Ephesians itself.

A Case Study. This scenario may seem far-fetched in North America, but it's very plausible in many parts of the world. In countries where Hinduism and Buddhism are prevalent, for example, the numerous temples and shrines are surrounded by merchants. Such traders will provide offerings for devotees to give inside these places of worship or will make and sell souvenirs for visitors to take home with them. Each religion is also supported by highly skilled craftsmen who deal in images of deities and spirits or who paint or provide specialized art and architectural details. When Christianity makes inroads in such places, the economy of local communities often experience the same dynamic felt by Demetrius and the Ephesian artisans. The threat is made more acute by the fact that religious traders frequently see their profession as a means of earning merit and divine favor. Any loss in business is perceived not only to affect their income but also their afterlife.

Session 2

Ephesians 1:17–19a. Consider having each group member pray this passage for another member every day for the next week, inserting his or her name in place of the "you" pronouns. Then at the end of the week, have everyone rotate to another member. In a few weeks, go back to the passage and see how God might have been answering your group's petitions for each other.

A Case Study. If someone in your group was adopted later than early childhood, you may want to ask how long it took him/her to feel like part of the family. The personal experience of being taken into a new home will make the message of this passage much more real to your group.

Session 3

A Case Study. After discussing the *Imagine* scenario, you may want to read Revelation 7:9–12 and make the point that the fictitious scene in this case study won't be fictitious at all one day. Every believer will get to experience it.

Session 4

Ephesians 3:20. A suggested application of this verse could be to encourage group members as they pray this week to ask God to show them how verse 20 applies to their life. At the next session, ask members for any insights they gained from praying about this truth and listening to God's Spirit.

Session 5

Suggested Application. Encourage participants to think of at least three ways they can go against the grain of the culture around them—and then do them this week.

A Case Study. This scenario lends itself particularly well to a two-sided debate. One team could argue for Christians separating themselves from the corruptions of the world while the other team defends the need to be involved in the world's cultures and systems.

Session 6

Suggested Application. If any participants are married (or about to be), encourage them to talk with their spouse/fiancée this week about how they can make their marriage a good picture of Jesus and the church.

Session 7

Suggested Application. Encourage participants to adopt a person outside of the group to pray for—someone whose struggles they know something about—and begin regular, persistent prayer for that person. If members will follow the trajectory of this person's battles over time, they will be able to see how they had a hand in the victories.

Session 8

Suggested Application. Urge members to choose someone they wouldn't normally associate with in their congregation or circle of acquaintances and then do something for him or her this week that demonstrates love.

Bibliography

Arnold, Clinton E. *Power and Magic: The Concept of Power in Ephesians*. Eugene, OR: Wipf & Stock, 1989.

———, ed. *Zondervan Illustrated Bible Backgrounds Commentary*. Grand Rapids: Zondervan, 2002.

Chilton, David. *Days of Vengeance: An Exposition of the Book of Revelation*. Fort Worth, TX: Dominion Press, 2006.

Closson, Don. "Paul and the Mystery Religions." <http://www.leaderu.com/orgs/probe/docs/mystery.html> (accessed July 13, 2008).

Kaiser, Walter C., Jr., and Duane Garrett, eds. *Archaeological Study Bible*. Grand Rapids: Zondervan, 2006.

Keener, Craig S. *The IVP Bible Background Commentary: New Testament*. Downers Grove, IL: InterVarsity Press, 1993.

Nee, Watchman. *Sit, Walk, Stand*. Carol Stream, IL: Tyndale House, 1957.

Witherington, Ben, III. *The Letters to Philemon, the Colossians, and the Ephesians: A Socio-Rhetorical Commentary on the Captivity Epistles*. Grand Rapids: Wm. B. Eerdmans, 2007.

———. *Revelation*. Cambridge: Cambridge University Press, 2003.

WALK THRU THE BIBLE®

Helping people everywhere
live God's Word

For more than three decades, Walk Thru the Bible has created discipleship materials and cultivated leadership networks that together are reaching millions of people through live seminars, print publications, audiovisual curricula, and the Internet. Known for innovative methods and high-quality resources, we serve the whole body of Christ across denominational, cultural, and national lines. Through our strong and cooperative international partnerships, we are strategically positioned to address the church's greatest need: developing mature, committed, and spiritually reproducing believers.

Walk Thru the Bible communicates the truths of God's Word in a way that makes the Bible readily accessible to anyone. We are committed to developing user-friendly resources that are Bible centered, of excellent quality, life changing for individuals, and catalytic for churches, ministries, and movements; and we are committed to maintaining our global reach through strategic partnerships while adhering to the highest levels of integrity in all we do.

Walk Thru the Bible partners with the local church worldwide to fulfill its mission, helping people "walk thru" the Bible with greater clarity and understanding. Live seminars and small group curricula are taught in over 45 languages by more than 80,000 people in more than 70 countries, and more than 100 million devotionals have been packaged into daily magazines, books, and other publications that reach over five million people each year.

Walk Thru the Bible
4201 North Peachtree Road
Atlanta, GA 30341-1207
770-458-9300
www.walkthru.org

Read the entire Bible in one year, thanks to the systematic reading plan in the best-selling **Daily Walk** devotional.

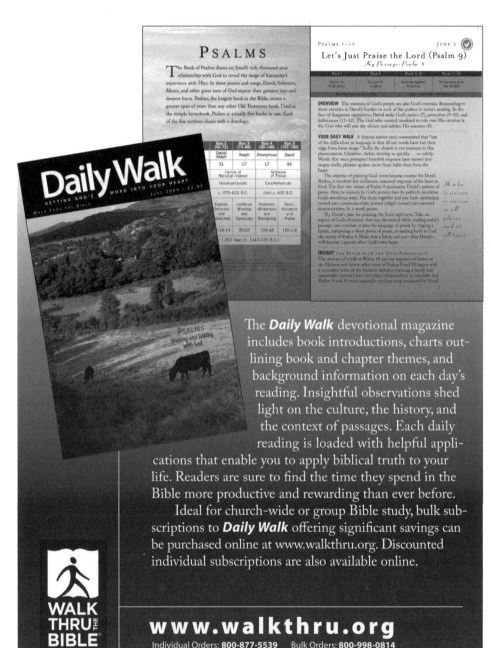

The **Daily Walk** devotional magazine includes book introductions, charts outlining book and chapter themes, and background information on each day's reading. Insightful observations shed light on the culture, the history, and the context of passages. Each daily reading is loaded with helpful applications that enable you to apply biblical truth to your life. Readers are sure to find the time they spend in the Bible more productive and rewarding than ever before.

Ideal for church-wide or group Bible study, bulk subscriptions to **Daily Walk** offering significant savings can be purchased online at www.walkthru.org. Discounted individual subscriptions are also available online.

WALK THRU THE BIBLE

www.walkthru.org

Individual Orders: **800-877-5539**   Bulk Orders: **800-998-0814**